THE SHARK

Look for these and other books in the
Lucent Endangered Animals and Habitats series:

The Elephant
The Giant Panda
The Oceans
The Rhinoceros
The Shark
The Whale

Other related titles in the Lucent Overview series:

Acid Rain
Endangered Species
Energy Alternatives
Environmental Groups
Garbage
The Greenhouse Effect
Ocean Pollution
Oil Spills
Ozone
Pesticides
Population
Rainforests
Recycling
Vanishing Wetlands
Zoos

THE SHARK

BY ADAM WOOG

Endangered Animals & Habitats

LUCENT BOOKS, INC.
SAN DIEGO, CALIFORNIA

Library of Congress Cataloging-in-Publication Data

Woog, Adam, 1953–
   The shark / by Adam Woog.
       p.   cm. — (Endangered animals & habitats)
   (Lucent overview series)
   Includes bibliographical references and index.
   Summary: Presents an overview of various species of sharks,
how they have become endangered, and what is being done to
protect them from extinction.
   ISBN 1-56006-462-5 (alk. paper)
   1. Sharks—Juvenile literature.   2. Endangered species—
Juvenile literature.   [1. Sharks.   2. Endangered species.]
I. Title.   II. Series.   III. Series: Lucent overview series.
QL638.9.W66   1998
597.3—dc21   97-21348
                                                      CIP
                                                      AC

Copyright © 1998 by Lucent Books, Inc.
P.O. Box 289011, San Diego, CA 92198-9011
Printed in the U.S.A.

Contents

Introduction

SHARKS ARE THE most powerful hunters in the sea. They live relatively long lives. They have virtually no natural enemies. They are almost perfectly adapted to their environment. They rarely even get sick. With all this going for them, sharks might seem to be immune from threats of any kind.

And yet, after thriving for over 400 million years as the top predators in their undersea world, some species of sharks are in danger of becoming extinct. This is a very recent development. Only thirty years ago, experts were confidently saying that sharks were in no danger at all, predicting that they would always roam the seas. In a book written in 1970, Jacques-Yves Cousteau, the undersea explorer and environmentalist who has probably done more than anyone to awaken the public to the wonders of marine life, states this view emphatically: "The majority of [sharks] are perfectly adapted to their mode of life and their enormous number makes their extermination extremely difficult, if not impossible."

Today, the story has changed dramatically. The populations of some species of sharks have fallen to such a low point that recovery is doubtful. More species will soon face a similar danger.

Experts have three rough categories of extinction for creatures that humans hunt or fish. The first is recreational extinction, meaning that sports enthusiasts cannot go hunting or fishing with any reasonable hope of success. The second is commercial extinction, meaning in the case of

aquatic creatures that industry-based fishing is so difficult and expensive that it is not worth the effort. The third is biological extinction, meaning that extermination is complete and no individuals of the extinct species exist.

After surviving for hundreds of millions of years as the most powerful predators in the sea, sharks are now becoming dangerously close to extinction.

Several species of sharks already fall into the first two categories, and experts fear the final category may be close at hand. According to environmental journalist Ted Williams, "Recreational extinction . . . and commercial extinction . . . are already facts for many shark species, and biologists are even talking about biological extinction for some."

Once worthless, now valuable

The species of sharks that are in the gravest danger include the great white shark, mako shark, dusky shark, sandbar shark, gray nurse shark, hammerhead shark, tiger shark, and lemon shark.

The drop in numbers for all these species has been steep and rapid. Speaking of shark populations along the east

Overfishing is responsible for the decline in population of many species of sharks including the lemon shark.

coast of the United States, Jack Musick, a shark expert at the Virginia Institute of Marine Science, remarks,

> The overwhelming trend . . . has been a massive decline that started somewhere in the early eighties. Right now [1996] the number of dusky sharks is probably ten percent of what it was in 1980. Sandbars are probably fifteen to twenty percent. Tigers are twenty to twenty-five percent. Same is true of sand tigers.

The main reason for this sudden change in the fortunes of sharks is an explosion of commercial fishing that specifically targets them. Sharks were for many years scorned by commercial fishermen as little more than "trash fish," marine garbage that was useful only as crab bait. Today, however, sharks are so valuable that hunting them has become big business.

The surge of interest in the commercial hunting of sharks is due to several factors. One reason is overfishing of other varieties of fish that are more popular for eating, such as cod, haddock, and tuna. As these species are approaching commercial extinction, the big fishing fleets are increasingly turning their attention to sharks.

Another reason is new medical, cosmetic, and industrial uses being found for products, such as oil and cartilage, that come from sharks. And a third reason for the explosive growth of shark hunting is the recent surge in China's economic strength and buying power: shark fins are valuable, expensive food items in Asia, and the worldwide harvesting of fins alone is now worth over a billion dollars a year.

Fear of sharks

Just as sharks have been hunted by humans for thousands of years, so have they terrified humans. Stories of savage shark attacks are as old as recorded history. Indeed, the English word "shark" comes from *schurke*, a German word meaning "ruthless villain" or "greedy parasite." Thus, even the creature's name reflects an image of mindless, consuming terror. As Philippe Cousteau, a son of Jacques-Yves Cousteau, remarks, "Second in violence only to the monstrous fury of hungry sharks is the blind hatred of man for this species."

To a degree, this reputation has survived to modern times. The chilling images of the man-eating great white shark in *Jaws*, the best-selling novel that became an even bigger movie in the mid-1970s, may be the only conception that people have about the creatures.

However, the reality is quite different. Humans have little to fear from sharks. Only about 35 of the approximately 350 species of sharks are considered a danger to people at all. Only a handful of these, meanwhile, represent a threat to most people. This is because many species of potentially dangerous sharks live in the deeper parts of the ocean, far away from any land. Only the few that live close to shore pose a threat to the general public. Jack Musick of the Virginia Institute of Marine Science puts it plainly: "Sharks are in a hell of a lot more danger from man now than *Homo sapiens* are in danger from sharks."

Sharks 25, humans 100 million

About 25 people are killed every year by sharks worldwide. Clearly, a person's chances of dying from a shark attack are very slim: one in 300 million, to be specific. To put this number into perspective, consider some other statistics. The odds of being killed by lightning are one in 2 million; of dying from a bee sting, one in 5.5 million; of being killed by falling airplane parts, one in 10 million. A person is much more likely to be killed in a car or airplane crash.

A great white shark surfaces to snap some bait between its powerful jaws. Though sharks pose only a relatively small threat to humans, they have been feared as ruthless man-eaters for thousands of years.

Humans, meanwhile, kill about a hundred million sharks every year. This figure includes only sharks killed by commercial or sport fishing; it does not count the untold numbers of sharks accidentally killed in drift nets or affected by pollution and habitat destruction. All these factors have been created by humans. In the words of Rodney Steel, a British expert on sharks:

> Sharks have few real enemies, save Man himself. . . . [T]he threat to sharks that is now posed by the advance of what purports to be civilisation—environmental pollution, excessive exploitation for sport and by commercial fisheries, habitat destruction, and simple . . . hunting down of what are popularly regarded as dangerous and undesirable killers could mean that the future of at least some shark species is already at stake.

Unless steps are taken quickly to protect sharks, experts like Steel warn that extinction will come soon, followed by serious repercussions for the environment as a whole.

1

What Makes a Shark a Shark?

SHARKS ARE FISH, and they share with all fish certain basic characteristics. They live in water. They are cold-blooded. And they get the oxygen they need to survive by inhaling water through sets of gills. However, except for these basic shared traits, sharks are very different from other fish.

In the same way, the 350 or so species of sharks in the world are remarkably different from each other. Despite a few common characteristics, there is a great deal of variety among individual shark species. Richard Ellis, an expert on undersea life, writes that "there are as many differences between a mako and a nurse shark as there are between an eagle and a sparrow."

Because most sharks live in the deep sea and researchers have not found a way to keep sharks in captivity for long periods, precious little is known about the details of the biology and behavior of these fascinating creatures. Still, increasing amounts of information have become available as technology has improved. According to British authority Rodney Steel, "Hauling sharks out of the sea on fishing lines and simply identifying their carcasses, which was about all that nineteenth- and early twentieth-century naturalists could hope to do, [have been] replaced by proper studies of shark behaviour and analysis of their physiology."

Sharkish characteristics

Scientists classify plants and animals, according to their characteristics, into various groups and subgroups. Along with skates, rays, and sawfish, sharks belong to the group that biologists call elasmobranchs. (The -*branch* comes from the Greek word for "gill," not the English "branch," and the plural is pronounced ee-LAS-mo-branx.)

Elasmobranchs differ in two basic ways from other fish. One is that they have more than one pair of gill slits. Some have many pairs, such as the appropriately named six-gill and seven-gill sharks.

The other major difference is that elasmobranch skeletons are made not of bone but of flexible cartilage. Indeed, a shark's skeleton bends so easily that, in the words of writer Doug Perrine, it is "quite easy for a shark to put its head back around by its tail—much to the chagrin [regret] of those [divers] who pull them."

Scientists have no complete fossil records of sharks because minerals in the soil became stuck on the teeth of ancient shark corpses but not the cartilage. The teeth remained hard and became fossilized, but the nonbony cartilage rotted away. So, although sharks have existed for 400 million years—since long before the time of dinosaurs—most of what researchers know about prehistoric elasmobranch species comes from the fossilized remains of their teeth.

Different gills and bladders

Sharks differ from other fish in many other ways. One of these ways involves their gill muscles. Most fish have muscles to pump water through their gills even when they are resting. With a few exceptions, however, this is not true of elasmobranchs. Lacking these muscles, elasmobranchs must force water through their gills by constantly swimming. This is why sharks seem to be always restless and on the move. Only a few species, such as nurse sharks, are able to lie still on the ocean floor to wait for prey.

Also, most fish have swim bladders. These sacs inside the body can be inflated or deflated to allow the fish to

Since their skeletons are made of nonbony cartilage that eventually rots away, most of what researchers know about prehistoric sharks comes from the study of their fossilized teeth.

float at different levels in the water. For reasons that are not completely clear, however, sharks do not have swim bladders. It may be that their extraordinary livers compensate for this lack. Shark livers are unusually large and contain a large quantity of oil, which is lighter than water. Some researchers suggest that this reservoir of buoyancy-creating fluid may be enough to keep the sharks mobile and floating at any depth. The shark's extremely supple cartilaginous skeletons would help in this respect.

Cannibals from birth

Sharks also differ from other fish in the ways in which they give birth. The female of most kinds of fish lays millions of eggs on the ocean or lake floor and the male fertilizes them afterward. Sharks have several methods of producing young, however, depending on the species.

Some species lay eggs, which remain in special sacs until the shark pups, as they are called, are hatched. Sharks that give birth in this way, including horn sharks, cat-sharks, and whale sharks, are called oviparous. The usual number of eggs is eight or ten.

The young of other species, called viviparous sharks, develop much like mammals: they grow inside the female and are fed by a placenta. The pups live in the womb for up to two years and are born in litters ranging in size from two to twenty. Viviparous sharks include the blue shark, hammerhead shark, and basking shark.

And some species use a strange hybrid method that ensures that the pups are predators—cannibals, in fact—from birth. These species, which include the tiger shark, spiny dogfish, and mackerel shark, are called ovoviviparous. The females of ovoviviparous species develop twenty or more eggs, which begin to hatch while they are inside the womb. The first arrivals eat the mother's unfertilized eggs and later devour their weaker siblings. (Sharks are born with teeth.) Usually, only one or two pups survive this brutal birth process.

More differences

Within the rough grouping of elasmobranchs, sharks are further subdivided for scientific purposes into 8 orders. Within these orders are about 30 families, which are further divided into more than 350 species. The list of known shark species is by no means complete; 3 to 5 "new" ones are discovered every year.

Some characteristics are shared by almost every shark species. Almost all, for instance, have one or two dorsal (back) fins, a pair of pectoral (side) fins, and a single anal fin near the rectum. Also, the upper portion of a shark's tail fin is usually larger than the lower lobe.

Beyond these basics, however, the many species of sharks differ greatly from each other. This wide variety is an indication of how well sharks have adapted to different environments.

Sharks range in size from the world's largest fish, the whale shark, which can reach a length of 60 feet, to the little cigar shark, only half a foot long when fully grown.

Contrary to popular belief, most sharks are not large. The average length of a shark is about 4.5 feet, and only a few species ever grow longer than 6 feet.

Sharks are found in all the world's oceans and sometimes even in freshwater lakes and rivers. Some species, such as hammerheads, tigers, and bull sharks, prefer shallow reefs in warm tropical waters; others, such as the dogfish shark and the oceanic white-tipped shark, stay in the colder, deeper parts of the ocean. And blue sharks, threshers, basking sharks, and makos prefer the moderate temperatures of temperate regions.

Some species are able to live in several climates and appear to roam the seas fairly freely. Other species, such as the nurse shark, stay in one spot for virtually their entire lives. A few species have been known to travel long distances, and scientists think that the blue shark is the most widely traveled of all. One blue shark was tracked from New York to Spain, and another from England to Brazil. Not much is known about the details of how or why sharks travel, though as far as researchers know, no species migrates yearly.

What they eat

The varied diet of sharks provides another example of how widely the species differ. Some species, including the

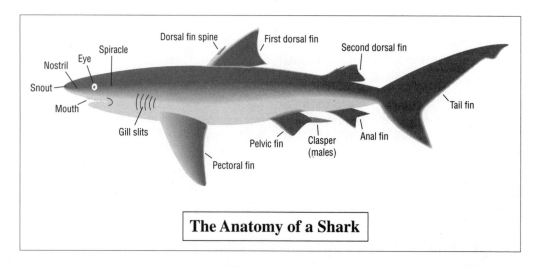

The Anatomy of a Shark

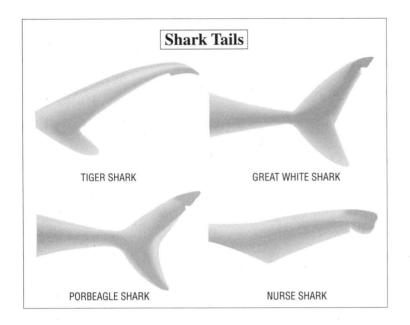

Shark Tails

TIGER SHARK

GREAT WHITE SHARK

PORBEAGLE SHARK

NURSE SHARK

great white and tiger shark, mostly eat large marine mammals, such as sea lions and killer whales. Tiger sharks will also eat large turtles and seabirds. Horn sharks, nurse sharks, and others that live on the ocean floor feed only on shellfish. Other species, such as hammerheads, favor small fish such as anchovies and medium-sized species such as stingrays, herring, cod, and salmon.

It is a myth that sharks are scavengers that will eat anything. Some species are extremely picky eaters; the sicklefin weasel shark, for instance, eats only squid and octopus. Under normal circumstances, in fact, most species are careful and selective about what they eat.

When regular food is scarce, however, sharks generally will eat whatever they can find. Parts of horses have been found in the stomachs of great white sharks, and in tiger sharks even stranger things have been discovered: bicycle parts, tin cans, overcoats, even a chicken coop complete with feathers and bones.

Sharks are almost unbelievably fast and limber when pursuing prey. Philippe Cousteau writes, "A shark's manner of eating is extraordinarily supple. He neither speeds toward the prey nor does he slow down; he seems simply

A black-tipped reef shark devours a mackerel. Sharks are usually selective about what they eat, contrary to the myth that they are scavengers.

to breathe in the portion he has chosen, which disappears into his still-opened mouth as he passes on."

Born to prey

Sharks have many specialized characteristics that are of special help in their continuing role as top predators in the open sea or in shallower waters. Among these are their jaw shape, skin, and teeth. In addition, sharks can swim more quickly and turn more sharply than many of their prey, athletic abilities that are due to their flexible skeletons. As Rodney Steel notes, "They [are] some of the most efficiently adapted of all fish, specialised to meet the demands of a hunter's life in the seas, with different species capable of exploiting environments as diverse as inland lakes and the ocean deeps."

The shark's efficiency in swimming and hunting is also enhanced by the protection and streamlining of its skin. Sharkskin is like armor, consisting of tiny plates made of the same material as shark teeth. Nature writer Doug Perrine describes these plates by stating that "they derive from the same embryonic tissue as the teeth, and each supports a tiny backwards-pointing tooth." Sharkskin is so rough to the touch that if it is stroked in the wrong direction, it can cause serious abrasion (scraping) injuries. The individual plates are joined together in a tight, seamless mesh that lets the shark move smoothly through the water.

The design of a shark's head is also a help as it preys on other sea life. Unlike most animals, both its upper and lower jaws are movable. This means that despite the long snout typical of many sharks, a hunting shark can attack a target head-on, without having to turn to the side to tear off a large section of flesh.

Teeth

Shark teeth are unique to each species, with each kind being well equipped for its particular diet.

Great white sharks, for instance, have broad and extremely sharp teeth, serrated like a bread knife. Such teeth are especially suited to tearing large chunks of flesh from prey. Basking sharks and whale sharks, meanwhile, have thousands of tiny teeth, which help them strain their food, tiny organisms called plankton, in the same manner as some species of whales. And the tiny cookie-cutter shark opens its semicircular jaws entirely and takes small, neat round bites out of its much larger prey. According to Doug Perrine, "The crater-like wounds it leaves are commonly seen on oceanic dolphins, whales and large pelagic [deep-sea] fish."

Sharks have several rows of teeth, although only the front row is used at a given time. Behind the front row of teeth are several rows of backups. These lie flat until they are needed, and then move forward to replace front teeth that break off or become lost. "A shark may have dozens to hundreds of teeth in its mouth at once," Perrine notes, "and go through thousands in a lifetime."

The smell of blood

Several complex sensory systems help sharks find prey quickly. A shark's ability to sense vibration, movement, and living things in the water is so sharp that it can easily distinguish between a healthy fish (one that might be difficult to catch) and an injured fish (one that may make an easier meal). These abilities are especially useful in locating injured fish. "Sharks race in from great distances to devour any fish in trouble," Jacques-Yves Cousteau writes. "They can perceive the fish's convulsive movements by the rhythm of the pressure waves carried to them through the water."

Their hearing is very sharp, and their ability to smell is also extremely good. Studies have shown that some species can smell another sea creature a quarter of a mile away.

A close-up of a sand tiger shark reveals its mouth full of sharp, pointed teeth.

Sharks can also sense changes in water pressure, and they have a further sense that is apparently unique to them, namely, the ability to detect electric currents in the water. All living creatures give off electricity, and it is a considerable advantage to a predator to be able to identify the source of such emissions. A shark can get a fix on a particular fish from as much as a hundred feet away.

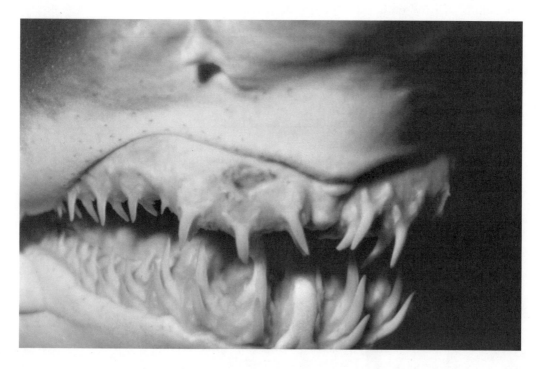

Scientists once thought that sharks had poor eyesight. However, they now believe that most species see very well indeed, using this ability primarily as they get closer to their prey. The eyes of sharks have reflectors, like cats' eyes, that magnify existing light. They are therefore well adapted to working in the dark.

Slow eaters, feeding frenzies

Typically, sharks eat surprisingly little. Because sharks cannot predict when they will encounter a food source, and so cannot rely on a steady and regular diet, they have adapted to a "feast or famine" routine. That is, they gorge themselves whenever possible and go without eating as necessary.

When a shark goes for a long period without eating and then breaks its fast, it can eat up to fifteen pounds in a single session. Sharks have been observed surviving for a month between meals, but evidence suggests that an average interval is two to three days.

One reason for this habit of eating sparingly is that sharks are so streamlined; being highly efficient swimmers, they need relatively little energy. Another reason is that the livers of sharks (which can account for a quarter of an animal's body weight) convert food into a highly nutritious oil, which provides a self-contained, timed-release source of calories.

A third reason is that sharks digest very slowly. This is particularly true of the many species that have a lengthy spiral valve through which their food moves during digestion. "Food passes through the valve extremely slowly, taking several days," explains Doug Perrine. "This slow digestive rate means the shark cannot feed often."

A dramatic characteristic of the eating habits of sharks is the so-called feeding frenzy. There is some uncertainty regarding the reasons for this phenomenon. Jacques-Yves Cousteau comments: "When sharks are gathered together in a group, their behavior is unpredictable. A 'frenzy' may suddenly take place, for reasons of which we still know nothing."

A group of sharks in a frenzy will tear into prey with ter-rifying speed and strength. They will also attack ship pro-pellers, hulls, diving cages, and other objects that are clearly not food; as the elder Cousteau remarks, "Sharks are accustomed to attacking, without fear, anything that floats." This may be because the metal in man-made objects has enough electricity to trigger the sharks' extremely sensitive mechanisms of detecting electric current. Thus, some ex-perts suggest that frenzies are not strictly due to hunger.

The dangerous ones

Sharks are large predators, and some sharks, under cer-tain circumstances, do pose a danger to unsuspecting or careless swimmers and divers. In the popular imagination, the most dangerous species is the great white shark—the one that was featured in *Jaws*. However, a greater number of attacks has been attributed to tiger sharks and bull sharks. Like the great white, these species tend to live near coast-lines. Experts also consider the oceanic black-tipped shark extremely dangerous because (unlike most species) it never flees from humans. However, since it lives only in the deep sea, it does not normally come in contact with people.

In some ways, it is surprising that shark attacks do not occur more often. After all, these large animals have been successful predators for millions of years. It would seem to be natural for a hungry shark to attack a person who en-ters its feeding territory. And yet the attack rate remains tiny, compared with the number of people who swim in the ocean. About 8 million people a year swim off Hawaii's beaches. The attack rate in the state of only 2.4 per year, however, indicates that sharks do not seek out humans as prey.

Evidence strongly suggests that sharks do not like to eat people. Apparently, they simply don't like the way hu-mans taste. Sharks such as the great white sometimes take bites out of people, perhaps mistaking a swimmer or surfer for a sea lion or other normal prey, but in virtually every recorded case, the shark has spit out the flesh and left the scene without biting again. Of course, a single bite from a shark can be serious, even fatal, but the image of these creatures as fierce man-eaters seems to be largely based in legend.

Sharks and biodiversity

Some people may ask why such dangerous and terrifying creatures are worth saving. Conservationists and researchers have come to the conclusion that a shortage of sharks in the future will have serious effects on the ocean, on the earth, and ultimately on people.

All wild animals, experts maintain, are vital to the health of the environment as a whole. Every plant and animal plays a particular role in maintaining biodiversity— that is, in keeping its particular ecosystem balanced. Upsetting that balance by removing even a small or seemingly unimportant species can have widespread and long-lasting effects. Conservationists stress that this concept applies to sharks as well, because they, as writer Jane Bosveld puts it, "like all the earth's living creatures, are anything but dispensable."

Conservationists argue that sharks play an especially important part in maintaining the complex pattern of biodiversity in the ocean. They do this in a way that illustrates the principles of natural selection. Sharks are so-called top or apex predators; that is, like lions and tigers on land, sharks are at the top of the marine food chain and live by feeding on weaker, slower animals. Like other top predators, sharks tend to search out the weakest animals they can find in a nearby group. By killing sick individuals and removing their remains from a given area, sharks help prevent the spread of diseases within the local population. Thus the general population of these species, called prey species, tends to be healthier.

"Sharks help control disease in fish populations," according to Dr. Samuel Gruber, a professor at the University of Miami and one of the world's leading shark experts. "They [also] play an important role in the evolution of prey species, taking the sick and unhealthy fish, leaving the more fit to breed." If the strongest individuals

Experts consider the black-tipped shark to be dangerous to humans, but because it lives in the deep sea, few people ever come in contact with this species.

in a species are the only ones left to reproduce, the stock of that species will remain strong over time.

The Great Plains and the sea

Gruber and other researchers worry that if sharks disappear, the balance of life in the ocean will be seriously upset. Without sharks, they say there is a risk to the ecosystem of a chain reaction in which the populations of some former prey species, weakened but in large numbers, would explode out of control. Gruber uses an example from earlier in this century, when two natural predators of the Great Plains, wolves and mountain lions, came close to extinction. "The plains stopped being a place where the deer and the antelope played," he states, "and became a place where the deer and the antelope became sick and overgrazed and destroyed their own habitat. The same thing can happen in the sea."

If it does, Gruber and other experts maintain, the fish once eaten by sharks will increase in number, but also will be weaker and sicker. In time, this trend could lead to the seas being dominated by very numerous fish unable to sustain themselves on the available amounts of food. Writer Doug Perrine summarizes the situation with this observation:

> In the ocean we are not sure what all the consequences of removing the apex predators from the food pyramid might be. We do have one example, though. A shark fishery in Tasmania collapsed after two years of overfishing. Shortly afterwards, the fishery for spiny lobsters also collapsed and fishermen observed a lot of octopus in the area. Octopuses are both major predators of spiny lobster and an important food item for sharks. It seems that once the numbers of octopus were no longer controlled by the sharks, they became too numerous and decimated [wiped out] the lobsters.

The effects of having fewer sharks in the sea are being felt in other parts of the world as well. In the waters off Florida, for instance, hammerhead sharks have been hunted into near extinction. Consequently, there has been an explosion in those waters in the number of stingrays, on which the hammerheads once preyed. One result of this change in the ecosystem has been an increase in the number of attacks on humans—by stingrays.

Over millions of years, sharks have developed their specialized senses and other characteristics to an astonishing degree, becoming almost perfectly suited to their lives as ocean predators. In the words of naturalist R. D. Lawrence, sharks are "creations that have adapted so wonderfully to their oceanic world that I consider them to be the most physically perfect of all life forms to be found on land or in the sea." Unfortunately, even these superior characteristics have not been enough to save sharks from their most serious threat: hunting by humans.

2

Hunting Sharks

HUMANS HAVE ALWAYS hunted for animals, on land and at sea. Not until modern times, however, have mechanized methods made hunting and fishing extremely efficient. And only very recently has fishing become efficient enough to put entire species of sea creatures, including sharks, in danger of extermination.

For thousands of years, people the world over took advantage of the ocean's seemingly endless bounty. In the last few decades, however, the available quantities of many of the most popular kinds of fish, such as tuna, have dropped alarmingly. Some experts fear that there literally may not be enough fish in the sea. As journalist Michael Parfit observes, "The unthinkable has come to pass: The wealth of oceans, once deemed inexhaustible, has proven finite, and fish, once dubbed 'the poor man's protein,' have become a resource coveted—and fought over—by nations."

Sharks are part of this increasingly scarce bounty. Today, commercial fishermen are responsible for the deaths of about a hundred million sharks every year. That is roughly 1.5 billion pounds of fish—enough to circle the globe more than four times if the dead sharks were laid end to end.

"Bycatch" is the term used to describe marine life-forms trapped by fishermen looking for certain other species. Deaths due to bycatch account for a large percentage of shark fatalities annually. In fact, some experts say that the majority of sharks killed by humans die in this way, and are therefore wasted, since most of the animal is

not eaten or otherwise used by people. Recreational or sport fishing is responsible for additional shark deaths, though the percentage is much smaller.

Commercial fishermen often inadvertently trap sharks in their nets while fishing for other species.

Commercial fishing

The amount of targeted shark fishing—that is, commercial fishing aimed specifically at sharks—has increased rapidly everywhere in recent years, with U.S. waters being no exception. In 1979 about 300,000 pounds of shark were caught in U.S. waters. Just ten years later, that figure had grown to 16 million pounds, and it is still climbing, despite efforts by conservationists to slow the trend.

To a large degree, this growth in the amount of shark meat caught by commercial enterprises is occurring because fishermen have overfished so many other kinds of fish, depleting their numbers to the point of commercial extinction. Even the most commonly eaten and formerly plentiful fish, like haddock and tuna, are no longer available

As populations of smaller fish are decreasing, commercial fishermen are increasingly turning to shark fishing. As a result, some shark species are already commercially extinct in some areas.

in unlimited quantities, and it is becoming increasingly expensive and difficult to find them. As a result, fishermen are turning to varieties of sea creatures—including sharks—that they once ignored.

Modern technology has also aided in the boom in shark fishing by enhancing the speed and efficiency of commercial fishing fleets. Improvements in shipbuilding and navigational equipment now enable large fishing boats to go virtually anywhere in the world, not just close to shore as in earlier times. The new technology also lets the large oceangoing operations catch more and more varieties of deep-water sharks that were once too difficult to find. These floating slaughterhouses move easily from one area to another as local shark populations become scarcer.

Because of the increasing demand for sharks, and because of the increased ease in finding them, fishermen have begun to overfish existing shark populations. Along the eastern seacoast of the United States, populations of duskies and sandbars are already commercially extinct because of overfishing.

Basking and porbeagle populations decline

Even when protected, the depleted shark populations can recover only very slowly, if at all; experts say that commercial extinction of a population is often followed by biological extinction. As Miami's Samuel Gruber points out, "Historically, when shark species are fished, they are wiped out, often within five years."

For example, there was once a thriving population of basking sharks in the North Atlantic. Basking sharks are prized for their livers, which can weigh half a ton or more, yielding large quantities of oil. In colonial times, however, fishermen virtually eliminated the populations along the eastern seaboard of the United States. By the middle of the twentieth century, basking sharks had also disappeared from Canadian waters and the northeastern Atlantic.

A more recent example is provided by the porbeagle or mackerel shark, a fast-moving deep-sea species similar to the mako and the great white shark. By the 1960s, less than a decade after being targeted by Norwegian and Japanese fishing fleets, the once plentiful Northwest Atlantic porbeagle became too scarce to hunt. Although fishing for Northwest Atlantic porbeagle stopped thirty years ago, the population has not recovered.

The problem of overfishing is made worse by the fishing industry's practice of indiscriminate catching. Commercial fishermen usually take females and young sharks as well as adult males. As a result, the number of sharks available to keep the reproductive cycle going is shrinking. In addition, only smaller, less desirable fish are available to breed new generations of the species. The population of female dogfish along the New England and mid-Atlantic coast, for instance, has been almost completely fished out, and for the last several years, fishermen there have mostly caught only medium-sized males.

Slow approach to reproduction

Another factor hindering the recovery of shark populations is the unusually long life cycle of most species. Not only do sharks live relatively long lives, ranging from twelve to seventy years depending on the species, but they generally do not reach sexual maturity, the time when they become able to reproduce, until they are between fifteen and thirty years old.

Other characteristics of shark biology add to the problem of late sexual maturity. Female sharks usually give birth only once a year; the rate is even lower in some species, such as once every two years for the sicklefin weasel shark. Moreover, the number of young produced by a female after each pregnancy is relatively small.

The infant mortality rate for sharks is high, as well: depending on the species, as many as 50 percent of all juveniles fail to live to adulthood.

Thus the survival of shark populations is by no means guaranteed by the general hardiness of the species. Many other kinds of fish can recover from overfishing because they reproduce rapidly and in large numbers. If left alone, for instance, a depleted population of flounder will double its size in a couple of years. A shark population of the same size, on the other hand, would take at least a couple of decades to return to the same level.

Many experts worry that the government agencies deciding fishing policies do not understand this crucial difference between sharks and other kinds of fish. Sonja Fordham, a spokeswoman for the Center for Marine Conservation, expresses this concern: "It's very disturbing that managers [of fish and wildlife conservation] don't differentiate. . . . [Sharks] are not cod; they don't start spewing millions of eggs at age two."

Desperately seeking sharks

Conservationists accuse the fishing industry of refusing to realize how serious the depletion of existing stocks has become. Fishermen, the conservationists argue, have more or less ignored the concept of a "sustainable yield," the idea of maintaining the population of sharks at a level that would enable them to reproduce sufficiently.

Instead of working toward this balance, critics say, fishermen are simply catching as many sharks as possible.

Then, when the sharks in a given area are gone, the fleets move on, like prospectors who have taken everything valuable from a mine. In Jack Musick's view, "Most of our fisheries have really been mining operations."

Conservationists argue that such shortsighted practices will ultimately be self-defeating. If shark populations are reduced to nothing, they reason, the industry will go the way of commercial whaling, which has virtually disappeared in recent years. As journalist Ted Williams writes, "Even considering nothing but humanity, as we always seem to do, the [idea of] liquidating the resource faster than it can reproduce seems insane."

Instead of focusing on finding alternatives, critics say, the industry is denying the findings of scientists who warn of dangerously low populations. A commercial fisherman based in North Carolina does not believe the dire predictions of marine biologists. His position, presented at a hearing conducted by a government agency, the Mid-Atlantic Fisheries Management Council, is as follows: "I look at the commercial fisherman's data as a hundred percent true. There are lies being used [by conservationists] to cause the alarm that the fish stocks are in trouble."

New targets

Meanwhile, the industry is also concentrating on finding new species to replace those that are gone. Among these new targets are deep-water species such as the wolf-fish shark, the spiny dogfish shark, and the grenadier shark (also called the rat-tail). Expensive, high-tech techniques will be required to capture such species, which live as far as three-quarters of a mile down in the ocean.

Defenders of large-scale shark fishing maintain that the industry is necessary to supply the world, especially developing countries, with raw material for manufactured products and with food. Critics, however, counter that most of the oil and other products humans take from sharks can be duplicated synthetically. As for shark meat, they say, the claim that developing countries need it is nonsense; the poorest countries do not receive the bulk of

Improved fishing techniques have enabled fishermen to catch deepwater species such as the spiny dogfish shark.

the catch. Farley Mowat, a prominent Canadian natural history writer and activist, sums up the conservationists' argument this way:

> The fishing industry of the developed nations, which is by far the largest and most destructive, achieves just the opposite result [from what it says]. Most of its production goes, not to starving peoples, but to those who are already the world's best fed, and who can afford high-priced food. . . . [A]s much as 40 percent of what could be used as human food is either completely wasted or is downgraded to make fish meal for animal feeds or fertilizer. On top of which . . . by commercially exterminating species after species of the more nutritious and abundant fishes in the sea, the modern commercial fishing industry is actually guaranteeing an increased burden of starvation for the hungry hordes who fill the human future.

Bycatch

There is persuasive evidence that the accidental harvesting known as bycatch endangers sharks even more seriously than overfishing by commercial fleets. Bycatch happens most commonly when sharks become entangled in nets or lines of fishermen trying to catch other species.

Experts at the National Oceanographic and Atmospheric Administration (NOAA) estimate that in American waters alone, about sixteen thousand metric tons of shark are lost as bycatch every year. This is more than twice the total allowable catch under guidelines established by the U.S. government in 1993. The total amount of bycatch worldwide is impossible to estimate.

Sharks are not the only kinds of fish affected by bycatch, but they are among those that are most severely affected. For one thing, their large, protruding fins and snouts make them especially vulnerable. Because of their size, they can easily get tangled in nets designed to catch smaller species.

Sharks cannot swim backward. Once caught, therefore, they cannot reverse course to free themselves. The less hardy species, such as hammerheads and tiger sharks, are especially vulnerable, as are any young sharks unable to use brute force to break through nets or snap fishing lines. It has been estimated that shrimp boats in southeastern U.S. waters alone catch and discard juvenile sharks totaling as much as three thousand tons annually. According to Charles Manire, a researcher at the University of Miami, the vast majority of shark deaths are due to bycatch: "Over 90 percent of all sharks caught [unintentionally by commercial fleets] are killed and then thrown back into the ocean to rot."

Throw them back?

Even when fishermen free trapped sharks from nets and return them to the sea alive, the fish are often so badly injured that they die soon afterward. The National Marine Fisheries Service has

A dead hammerhead shark hangs in a twisted fishing net. Experts believe that many shark deaths are due to bycatch.

estimated that only about half the sharks caught as bycatch and then released survive the ordeal.

Adding to the problem is the general indifference of fishermen toward helping trapped sharks. Sharks are seen as nasty nuisances and threats to the fleet, since they often are competing for the same kinds of fish the fishermen are after. They are also often dangerous to the fishermen, who tend to kill the creatures and throw the corpses back in the ocean, rather than embark on the risky task of freeing up angry or frightened sharks, incapable of understanding that someone is trying to help them.

Furthermore, commercial fishermen are under virtually no legal pressure to show mercy toward sharks. Though finning is banned in certain U.S. waters, sharks are not safeguarded by hunting laws, like those protecting dolphins and sea turtles. Thus, there are few penalties for those observed killing and discarding sharks. Restrictions on commercial catches apply in some areas, but they are virtually impossible to enforce.

Indiscriminate catches

Two fishing techniques, longline fishing and drift netting, are responsible for the majority of shark bycatch. Longlines are used to catch tuna, swordfish, and other large species of fish. Since these fish are often more valuable than sharks, fishermen who are not targeting sharks simply cut unwanted sharks off their lines. These sharks are often so severely injured by the process that they soon die.

Experts say that it is difficult to estimate exactly how many sharks are needlessly killed by longlines. However, studies indicate the numbers may be very high. One study by the marine laboratories of the Commonwealth Scientific and Industrial Research Organization, in Australia, found that just one fleet of Japanese tuna longliners off the coast of Tasmania accidentally killed 43,500 blue sharks in a single ten-year period. These blues were finned and then dumped back in the sea; that is, the valuable fins were cut off and the rest of the fish, still alive, was discarded.

Typically, a finned shark will quickly die. Sometimes, however, they survive the ordeal and continue to prey as best they can. "In 1987," journalist Ted Williams reports, "two contestants in a Florida fishing tournament reeled in finless tiger sharks that could only wriggle along the bottom and apparently had taken the cut bait because they couldn't catch anything that swam."

The other common fishing method responsible for large amounts of bycatch is drift netting. Huge nets, up to twenty-five miles long, are spread in the ocean behind fishing boats. As the nets drift with the current, enormous quantities of fish enter and eventually are pulled aboard the boats for harvesting.

Drift netting is indiscriminate. That is, drift nets cannot pick up one kind of sea creature and leave another behind. The giant nets simply bring in everything they catch. A drift-netting fleet that has fished an area out moves on to another location. Drift netting has been called "strip-mining of the sea" because of its destructiveness.

Any drift net bycatch is usually discarded, since space on the vessel is limited. Valuable shark fins may be saved,

A man sits among the tangles of his fishing net repairing a damaged section. Even if fishermen who inadvertently catch sharks in their nets return them to the sea, the fish are often so badly injured that they do not survive the ordeal.

but not the rest of the animal. Finned sharks are thrown back into the sea, where they almost surely die.

As with longline fishing, it is difficult to accurately guess the number of sharks caught by drift netting. However, Greenpeace Australia has estimated that during the mid-1970s, Taiwanese and Korean squid drift netters accidentally killed over 2.25 million blue sharks in a one-year period alone. And it has been estimated that the bycatch ratio for some kinds of net fishing, such as shrimping, is 4 to 1; in other words, fishermen catch (and discard) up to four times as many pounds of unwanted fish as they catch (and retain) of the targeted species.

Nets can create other kinds of hazard for sharks, including the so-called ghost nets, enormous plastic fishing nets that have been thrown away but do not biodegrade. Ghost nets float around in the ocean for years, and sharks that become entangled in them are trapped, unable to hunt or eat.

Safety netting used to protect ocean bathers from sharks also kills many sharks each year. These deaths are not intentional: The idea is to keep people from being hurt, not to kill sharks that happen to come to the area. Once sharks become entangled, however, they cannot continue to swim and soon die. According to one report, off the beaches of just one area, Queensland, Australia, 20,500 sharks died over the course of sixteen years. These nets remain, killing thousands of sharks and other animals, including dugongs (an endangered marine mammal), porpoises, sea turtles, and rays, each year.

Sport fishing

The exact number of sharks caught by recreational or sport fishermen is not available, but presumably it is relatively small compared to the number caught for commercial purposes. Still, sport fishing does contribute to the overall decline in shark populations.

Sport or recreational shark fishing has been common among enthusiasts for many years. Among the species of sharks regarded especially highly for their fighting abilities are the mako, porbeagle, white, thresher, and tiger sharks. Of these, the mako is probably the most commonly sought, and sport fishermen pay large fees to charter boat operators who are able to bring their customers to the heart of mako territory.

In the mid-1970s sport fishing for sharks soared in popularity, thanks to *Jaws*. A worldwide sharkmania throughout the 1970s resulted in hundreds of shark fishing contests, often called "monster hunts," with prize money in the tens of thousands of dollars offered for the biggest trophy caught.

These trends and practices have had predictable results. For instance, recreational shark hunting with mechanized weapons such as pneumatic harpoons nearly wiped out the shark populations off the southern Australian coast. Because of the wholesale killing, the once-common gray nurse shark is now protected in this region. Charter boat operators in Florida and other popular sport fishing locations have noticed similar declines in shark populations; where once a charter operator's clients might catch ten or

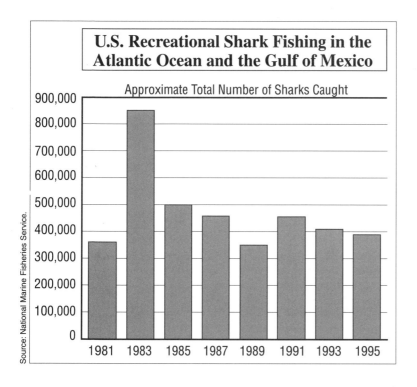

U.S. Recreational Shark Fishing in the Atlantic Ocean and the Gulf of Mexico

Approximate Total Number of Sharks Caught

Source: National Marine Fisheries Service.

twelve sharks in a day, now they consider themselves lucky to land a single one.

Sport fishermen have noticed a decline in the quality and size, as well as the quantity, of the fish they have caught in recent years. Simply put, the record catches of the relatively recent past are no longer attainable, probably because of overfishing. For example, the prize-winning fish in one large recent tournament was a relatively puny gray nurse shark. Whereas the average weight for that species is 200 to 250 pounds, the winner's catch weighed only about 60 pounds.

Under the circumstances, many charter boat operators have begun advocating limits to daily catches. Also, so-called catch-and-release fishing, in which lines are cut and sharks are released back into the water, is gaining in popularity with many charter fishing operations and shark tournament promoters. Pete Barrett, a writer who specializes in sport fishing, applauds this trend: "What pleases me is to see charter boats voluntarily imposing on themselves a limit of one mako, let's say, per day at a minimum of 250 pounds, or just catching and releasing sharks altogether."

Recreational fishermen proudly display their catch, a tiger shark, in this 1986 photo. Known as a fierce fighter, the tiger shark is especially prized by fishermen because of its difficulty to land.

Legislating the fishermen

In the 1980s, several groups concerned with the environment began working to pass laws limiting shark fishing. So far, however, efforts to enact a shark conservation plan, both internationally and in the United States, have been only partly successful.

Worldwide, the environmental movement has worked for several decades to pass laws designed to slow the trend toward the extinction of endangered species in general.

In 1973 many countries, including the United States, signed an agreement called CITES, which stands for Con-

vention on International Trade in Endangered Species of Wild Fauna and Flora. CITES designates certain species of animals as endangered (that is, in danger of becoming extinct) or threatened (that is, facing the possibility of endangerment if not protected). To protect endangered species, CITES imposes fines on hunters who kill them or developers who destroy their habitat.

However, the agency that governs CITES, the International Union for the Conservation of Nature (IUCN), is a slow-moving bureaucracy. Because it must deal with many factors, such as conflicting scientific data and the concerns of many different governments and interested groups, the agency cannot add species to the list as quickly as activists warn that they are becoming endangered.

The only sharks listed in the *Encyclopedia of Endangered Species*, a reference book printed in association with the IUCN, are the great white, the gray nurse, and the hammerhead. The many other shark species that are in danger are only a few of the many threatened animals that have yet to be recognized as officially endangered by the IUCN.

Currently, only a handful of local regulations exist in various countries to protect sharks. Laws protect the great white shark off the coasts of South Africa, for instance, and in southern Australia it is illegal to hunt the gray nurse shark.

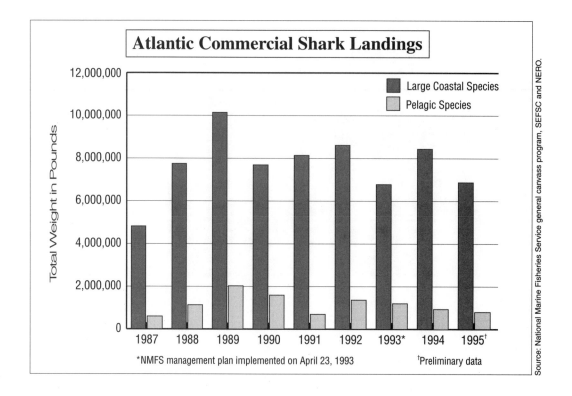

Atlantic Commercial Shark Landings

*NMFS management plan implemented on April 23, 1993   †Preliminary data

Source: National Marine Fisheries Service general canvass program, SEFSC and NERO.

The NMFS policy

The Endangered Species Act (ESA), a U.S. law with provisions similar to those of CITES, was passed in 1973. However, conservationists charge that the government has been too slow to respond to the shark situation. In fact, they complain, in many ways the government has fostered the harvesting of sharks. For years, for instance, the National Marine Fisheries Service (NMFS), a branch of the Department of Commerce, actively encouraged the fishing industry to target sharks as an alternative to other species that had been overfished.

In the late 1980s, under pressure from conservation groups like the Center for Marine Conservation, NMFS changed its policy and began to advocate management plans designed to control and sustain populations of sharks. It was not until 1993, however, that NMFS released its recommendations. This management plan, since put into effect, limits catches of thirty-nine species, outlaws the practice of finning, and sets other restrictions in the U.S. waters of the Atlantic, the Caribbean, and the Gulf of Mexico.

The commercial fishing industry reacted strongly against the plan, which they feel is unnecessary and unfair. The industry argues that the plan unjustly penalizes the American fishing fleet, inasmuch as other countries are not obliged to limit their catches. Critics within the industry also question the accuracy of the NMFS figures for existing shark populations. The true numbers, they say, indicate that sharks are not at all endangered.

NMFS shark coordinator Mike Bailey says that the plan "has gone a long, long way toward slowing down the shark fishery." However, while many conservationists

ROTHCO

THEY CONFISCATED MY WHOLE DAYS CATCH— A BOOT AND TWO TIRES

"You're in big trouble if you don't let that fish go—these are American waters!"

agree that the plan is a step in the right direction, they also find it limited and timid.

For one thing, they point out, the plan was concerned only with certain portions of U.S. waters. The Pacific was excluded from the NMFS plan, primarily because there is currently very little commercial shark fishing there. Since only 39 out of the more than 350 known species of sharks were specifically addressed, they also worry that many commonly hunted but unprotected species, such as dog-fish sharks, are in particular danger. Furthermore, concerned activists question the ability of the NMFS to effectively monitor and enforce its guidelines, even though agents of the agency make regular inspections of commercial fishing fleets.

A zero quota

Finally, the experts charge, the limits set by the plan are not low enough, and the recovery rates it predicts are unrealistically low. Carl Safina, director of the National Audubon Society's Living Oceans Program, is one of these critics. He advocates a zero quota on sharks—in other words, no legal fishing for sharks at all. Even if a zero quota is set in the next few years, however, Safina fears that sharks may never regain the numbers they once had. He concludes:

> The fact is that no shark scientist believes [the population] can recover to where it was in 1985 in less than several decades. In ten years we have dug a hole that will take half a century to get out of if we act now. . . . We can look forward to the benefits of recovery of striped bass, groundfish, even tuna. But we will never again see as many sharks as we had in the 1980s. This is a heart-breaking state of affairs.

Commercial fishing for shark may thrive for many years, despite the efforts of conservationists and others concerned with sharks' welfare. This will be especially true if people continue to perceive benefits from products made from sharks and from the many uses to which the meat, fins, and other body parts can be put.

3

How Sharks Are
Used by People

AT ONE TIME or another in history, people around
the world have put virtually every part of the shark to
some purpose. Sharks have been used extensively over the
years for food, for medicine, for fashion, and for products
such as oils that serve in manufacturing and other enterprises. Recently, the importance of sharks for manufacturing has dropped, but their value as food and as sources of
medicinal compounds has skyrocketed.

Sharks as food

People have always hunted sharks for food, and that is
one of the main reasons for the persistence of shark
hunting.

Although high in protein, shark is not the ideal food for
humans. Some species have meat that is inedible or unap-
petizing. All shark meat spoils quickly, so it is difficult to
ship and prepare well.

Still, many species of shark have flesh that is firm in
texture and delicious in taste. Shark has been a staple for
centuries in countries with cuisines and tastes as varied as
Italy, Vietnam, Jamaica, Mexico, Lebanon, Turkey, and
Java. Writer Kevin Sinclair remarks that early explorers
spread tales of eating roasted shark in coastal villages
around the world. "Greek and Roman gourmets ate shark
with enthusiasm and throughout the Mediterranean today
it is a delicacy in many a kitchen," he adds.

In America, however, the idea of shark as an item on restaurant menus has had difficulty catching on. At least one reason is not hard to surmise. "Why has a fish so universal, so plentiful, been regarded for so long by Western diners as distasteful?" asks Kevin Sinclair. "Presumably because of the fearsome reputation of the shark."

Another reason for the failure of shark to become popular in American cuisine has been the ready availability of other kinds of fish, such as red snapper, swordfish, and sea bass. As these species have become increasingly difficult to catch because of overfishing, however, commercial fishermen have discovered that shark can make an acceptable substitute.

Recently, for instance, the fish-and-chips market has increased its reliance on some elasmobranch species, especially the dogfish, to supply its needs. More upscale restaurants have also begun serving shark, though often by a different name, such as "flake" or "steakfish."

This effort to make shark more appealing in the marketplace has worked, perhaps too well; the lowly shark, once thought of as useful only as bait, is now a prized catch. As Sonja Fordham of the Center for Marine Conservation acknowledges, "One of the lessons we're learning is that today's trash fish is tomorrow's delicacy."

Shark fins

By far the most valuable part of any species of shark is its fins, which unlike the meat can be preserved by means of low-tech approaches such as salting and drying. Shark fin soup is a great delicacy in China, where shark fins also have been used for centuries in the making of traditional medicines.

The rapid growth of the Chinese economy and its booming trade with the outside world since the 1980s has brought an especially great demand for fins of almost any size or type. By 1990, over sixty countries were supplying Hong Kong and mainland China with nearly 5 billion pounds of fresh or dried shark fins every year.

The demand from Asia has sharply driven up the price of shark fins. Also contributing to the high costs are the increasing scarcity of sharks and the extremely labor-intensive process of making shark fin soup. Today, a single pound of dried shark fin can cost as much as $200. A bowl of shark fin soup can cost upward of $150 in a gourmet Chinese restaurant.

The ban on finning in some U.S. waters, imposed in 1993 by the NMFS, cuts down on the practice to some extent. Worldwide, though, finning results in the mutilation of millions of sharks every year and the waste of many tons of shark meat.

Skin, teeth, corneas, and more

Sharkskin has been used for centuries in human apparel and for weapons. Its toughness gives it value as a durable, high-quality leather for boots, purses, and other articles of clothing. The roughness of its surface is another useful property. According to

Shark fins are in great demand from Asian countries, where they are used as food and as an ingredient in traditional medicine.

shark expert José I. Castro, "In the past the dried-up skins of sharks, known as shagreen, were used as fine sandpaper. At one time shagreen was also used to cover the hilts of Japanese and German swords, since its rough surface provided a firm grip even when the hilt was bloodied."

Sharks' teeth have also had many uses. In Eskimo and South Sea societies they were used for spears, swords, and saws. During the Victorian era they served as decorations for men's watch chains in Europe and America. They still are somewhat popular jewelry items, seen in necklaces and chains.

The ancient Greeks, Romans, and Chinese used shark components extensively for their medicinal value. They recognized, for instance, that the livers of sharks, which are rich in vitamin A, provide an oil that makes people stronger.

Vitamin A has been synthesized chemically since the 1950s, all but stopping the use of shark oil as a source of this dietary supplement. But other organs and body parts are still used in a wide variety of medicines and cosmetics. For example, shark liver oil is a common ingredient in hemorrhoid ointments. Also, the livers of sharks are rich in a product called squalene that is a common ingredient in skin rejuvenators and other cosmetics.

Nearly every part of the shark has been put to use by humans. Recently, sharks have become highly valued as sources of food and medicinal products, giving fishermen more incentive to hunt them.

Recently, shark eyes have also been used for medical purposes. For reasons scientists do not understand fully, shark corneas are unusually strong; if scratched or ruptured, they show none of the damage that so readily affects the corneas of other creatures. Shark corneas have been successfully transplanted into humans. Sharkskin, also, has been shown to have a therapeutic use, as a temporary artificial skin for human burn victims.

Other still experimental medical uses for sharks involve the manufacture of medications to combat certain heart conditions and to control the coagulation, or thickening, of blood. These trials were begun on the basis of indications that sharks are rich in chemicals that lower cholesterol levels in heart tissues and slow the coagulation of the blood.

Immune system research

Other experiments in medical research may eventually provide the single most important reason for continuing to catch large quantities of sharks. Scientists are very interested in the possibility that sharks can supply answers to a number of serious medical puzzles, solutions to which would immensely benefit humankind.

Sharks have amazing immune systems. Despite living in oceans teeming with dangerous bacteria and viruses, sharks in the wild very seldom are seriously ill. In addition, they regularly eat diseased fish but rarely get sick. Researchers are intensely curious to know why this is so, since identifying the reason may show medical science ways to strengthen the human immune system, one of the body's most important defenses against disease.

Apparently, the key lies buried in time. In fossils of animals that evolved before sharks, hundreds of millions of years ago, scientists have found no trace of four specific proteins that are crucial to effective immune systems. However, in sharks and animals that developed after sharks—including bony fishes, amphibians, reptiles, birds, and mammals—all four proteins are present. This indicates that sharks may have been the first living creatures to possess complete and effective immune systems. "The way it looks today," says science writer Rosie Mestel, "sharks demark a great divide in the world of immunity."

Primitive simplicity

Sharks' immune systems are much simpler than those of humans, and in some ways are not as highly evolved. They reject tissue grafts more slowly than we do, for example, and quick rejection of skin grafts is seen as a later evolutionary characteristic, calling for a complex response on the part of the organism. In contrast, the hardiness of sharks may be linked to their simpler makeup. Researchers speculate that sharks are usually healthy because they combine primitive simplicity of bodily organization with the presence of the four key proteins not found in earlier life-forms.

Research in this area is only in the very beginning stages, and no one knows exactly what may come of it. Many scientists, however, hope that by studying the physical and chemical makeup of sharks, they will be able to unlock secrets that will help them fight AIDS and other serious diseases that affect human immune systems.

Researchers caution, however, that the search will take years and that the outcome is uncertain; no one knows what, if anything, the study of primitive immune systems will reveal about the workings of the human body. On the other hand, the results could be enormously important. Gary Litman, a researcher at All Children's Hospital in Saint Petersburg, Florida, expresses the guarded optimism of the research community: "Little we've ever done in the [shark immune] system has been predicted accurately by us—it's almost always been a surprise. But that's been the most exciting thing about it."

Can sharks cure cancer?

Pills made from shark cartilage have been the focus of considerable controversy. Some researchers claim that shark cartilage, the flexible skeletal material that distinguishes elasmobranchs from bony fishes, can cure cancer.

Shark cartilage pills have been touted as having the ability to slow the growth of cancerous tumors. Experts caution, though, that more research is needed to validate this claim. Meanwhile, the demand for shark cartilage is enormous.

The assertion has created an enormous worldwide fad for consuming pills containing shark cartilage. Despite a lack of hard evidence that these expensive pills help in any way, they are being bought in huge quantities by patients desperate for a cure, and by people who hope to receive preventive benefits. Shark cartilage harvesting has become so big, generating an estimated $50 million a year, that entire populations of sharks are in danger of extermination.

For example, the hammerhead populations off the coast of Costa Rica have been fished almost to extermination for their cartilage. According to journalist Catherine Dold, "The rationale is that sharks will be harvested for their meat and fins anyway. But there is little doubt that shark fishing is increasing as cartilage gains in popularity." Dold quotes Robert Hueter, the director of the Center for Shark

Research, as follows: "Without regulations or management, there is an absolute danger that this [Costa Rican] fishery will collapse very quickly. It can't last more than a couple of years."

The fad started in the 1980s when an American nutritionist named I. William Lane began studying the possibility that shark cartilage slows the growth of cancerous lesions [abnormal changes] in the organs and tissues of mice. Most U.S. cancer scientists and doctors dismissed his ideas, however, so Lane conducted tests on human patients in Cuba. He claimed in 1992 that twenty-nine terminally ill cancer patients started to respond after six weeks. Three and a half years later, fourteen of the patients were apparently cancer-free, while nine had died of cancer and six had died of other causes.

When Lane's Cuban experiments were featured on the television show *60 Minutes*, the demand for shark cartilage skyrocketed, both in America and elsewhere. Lane's book, *Sharks Don't Get Cancer*, became a best-seller. He and other entrepreneurs also grew wealthy by selling shark cartilage pills.

The role of blood flow in cancer

Lane's claims are based on an accepted medical principle. For a cancerous tumor to grow, it needs nourishment in the form of blood. In a process called angiogenesis, the tumor gets this nourishment by causing new blood vessels to form and grow toward it. In theory, if blood can be prevented from reaching a tumor, the growth will die.

Lane and other advocates of shark cartilage claim that the substance is anti-angiogenic; that is, that there is a substance in the cartilage that prevents blood vessels from developing. The presence of this substance, they say, explains why sharks rarely get cancer. Many doctors and researchers, however, are skeptical.

Although scientists agree that sharks appear to possess a chemical that inhibits the growth of blood vessels, hard evidence that this substance is responsible for the low cancer rate in sharks is lacking. Moreover, it has not been proved that humans who take the medicine will have a lower cancer rate.

Moral and ethical questions

Also, critics raise moral and ethical questions. They worry that desperate cancer victims are being misled with false hopes, so that they pay immense sums for pills considered to be worthless by most practicing oncologists (doctors who specialize in cancer). Samuel Gruber, the University of Miami shark expert, has tried many unusual cures in his own battle against cancer. However, he holds out no hope for shark cartilage. "I can understand the fear of somebody who is told there is nothing more that medicine can do for them, and the lengths they would go to," he remarks, "[but] I consider it a cruel hoax that . . . people are making money by killing sharks that don't need to be killed and by promising [patients] that they are going to get their cancer cured."

Even if an anticoagulant chemical from sharks could somehow affect the human bloodstream, researchers say, ingesting the substance in the form of pills would not be sufficient. Because of the way proteins are absorbed into the body, a person would have to eat hundreds of pounds of cartilage. Judah Folkman, a leading cancer researcher at Harvard Medical School, sums up the attitude of most of his colleagues: "I'll change my mind if I ever see any study that shows that it works, but we have solid scientific evidence that it couldn't."

Difficulties in shark research

The state of research on sharks—and on how sharks may help humans medically—is still relatively primitive. Because of the difficulty in studying the living creatures, shark scientists know surprisingly little about their subject. Large gaps remain in their understanding of even the most basic aspects of sharks' lives and behavior. Not much is known, for instance, about where adult sharks go when they are not spawning or feeding. As Samuel Gruber points out, "We *are* learning. But there is so much more that is unknown. . . . We only have the basic story, with a lot of holes in it."

In part, this lack of knowledge reflects the low priority of sharks in the minds of many scientists and politicians. Funds for research are therefore limited. In addition, there are fewer and fewer sharks to study. One of the biggest study groups in the world, centered at the University of Miami, was once easily able to catch, tag, and release two thousand lemon sharks in a single summer. Now, according to spokesman Charles Manire, the team is lucky to find thirty or forty in the same amount of time. A few years ago, the group moved its research station to the Caribbean island of Bimini because there were no longer enough sharks in south Florida's waters.

Another major problem in elasmobranch research is simply that the sharks are difficult to study. It is almost impossible to observe them in their natural environment. Most species of sharks have never even been photographed in their native habitat.

Many factors account for the difficulty of observing sharks in the wild. For example, despite recent improvements in underwater gear, the ability of humans to travel and function underwater is limited. Also, sharks are not easy to find. Some species travel from one area to another, or live only in remote areas. They are relatively swift swimmers, and most species shy away from human contact. Finally, there is the matter of safety: some species pose serious dangers to humans who come too near.

Sharks in captivity

These and other considerations make it virtually impossible to study individual sharks over long periods. John Paxton, a researcher at Australian Museum in Sydney, puts it this way: "We can't get down there [in the ocean] and be with them all the time. You can't put a tag on individuals and follow them through life." Whereas most sea creatures can be caught relatively easily and tagged with radio tracking devices, this is hardly the case with sharks.

Most aquarium animals are captured close to shore, and marine biologists are able to simulate their natural environments well enough to permit them to thrive in captivity. Many sharks, however, are deep-water animals and generally do very poorly in aquariums or other research facilities. In addition, most species require careful capture and transport, large holding areas, the highest water quality, and appropriate diets. Under the circumstances, perhaps it is not surprising that scientists have had little success in studying captured sharks.

Examples of the difficulties involved in doing research with captive sharks are not hard to come by. The new state-of-the-art wing of California's Monterey Bay Aquarium is a pioneering facility designed to re-create the open sea as much as possible. Yet two blue sharks scheduled for display there died shortly before the grand opening.

In order to study sharks more closely, marine biologists are designing aquariums that simulate ocean conditions. So far, however, the blue shark (pictured) has not thrived in captivity.

The second blue shark had been in the new wing for only a week. The cause of its death was uncertain, but digestive problems may have been to blame. According to Joe Choromanski, the aquarium's curator of husbandry operations, "Either [the shark] had a pre-existing condition when we caught him, or the stress of capturing him did something. We need to learn more. It's not like there are any veterinary textbooks on how to care for sharks." In any event, the record for keeping a blue shark in captivity is only seven months.

Further dangers

If biologists and other researchers can solve the problems involved in maintaining sharks in captivity, their success could have far-reaching results. Not only would they be able to study sharks more closely, accumulating information that could help human medical research, but they might be able to breed sharks in captivity. And the breeding in captivity of an endangered species can be an important part of its survival or extinction.

Until researchers can solve the riddles that prevent sharks from thriving under human care, the commercial hunting of the animals will probably continue. In the meantime, sharks face the dangers of pollution and habitat destruction.

4

Pollution and Habitat Destruction

FISHING IS THE single biggest threat to the well-being of sharks, but it is not the only one.

Virtually all animals have natural enemies—that is, other animals that prey on them. As top predators, sharks are generally free of this problem. Even so, small species of sharks, and juveniles that are not fully grown, are vulnerable to attacks from bigger sharks, as well as from other predators such as crocodiles and seals.

Killer whales and dolphins can also be threats to sharks. These mammalian species have been known to drive their bony snouts into the only soft, vulnerable parts of the sharks' bodies: their gill structures and underbellies. If a target shark is unable to swim safely away before it has been battered a few times in this way, it may weaken to the point of allowing the attackers to kill it.

A giant dumping area

A far greater threat to sharks than the occasional attack by other sea creatures is pollution. Even if fishing for sharks ended immediately, this human-made problem would continue to endanger their survival.

The earth's oceans are often the final dumping ground for the waste that civilization produces. For centuries, even experts assumed that ocean-dwelling creatures were relatively safe from harm because their habitat is so immense. Only recently have people begun to realize that chemicals

55

and other trash dumped into the ocean soon enter the food chain, often with devastating results. "When I was a student [in the 1950s], I thought the oceans were so wide and so vast that it was impossible to degrade the system," says Samuel Gruber. "I thought it was a great sink [dump] for chemicals and pollution, and there was no way to put a dent in the marine populations. Boy, was I wrong."

Very little is known about the direct effects of pollution on sharks. Again, this is largely because research on sharks and shark conservation has had a very low priority among most scientists and government agencies. The little that we do know indicates that sharks, being relatively hardy, are not as severely affected by pollution as other sea creatures, such as whales and tuna.

Typically, polluting chemicals in the water are picked up by simple organisms near the bottom of the food chain. These organisms, such as algae and plankton, are eaten by animals higher in the chain, and the bodies of the larger animals contain these chemicals in increasingly high concentrations. By the time animals as high on the food chain as whales and tuna eat polluted prey, the concentrations can be extremely heavy. Many of these higher species become seriously ill or even die as a result.

Since sharks are at the top of the ocean's food chain, they might be expected to show significant evidence of this pollution. Rarely, however, does exposure to toxic chemicals make sharks sick. Researchers believe that a powerful immune systems protects sharks from life-threatening substances present in the oceans.

Indirectly affected by pollution

However, sharks are indirectly affected by pollution. This is because any given species is affected by changes in the populations of other animals in the sea. As top predators, sharks depend on other fish for food. If those fish are scarcer because pollution has reduced their numbers, or if the population of healthy fish drops substantially, sharks will have less to eat and will suffer accordingly.

ROTHCO

Pollution from toxic waste first affects sea life at very basic levels. A typical example occurs when nitrogen and phosphorus, common by-products of industry, are dumped into an ocean, or into a river that empties into a coastal ecosystem. The presence of these chemicals triggers an explosive degree of growth among microscopic plants. Yet as these nearly invisible organisms die and decompose, they both cause a sharp drop in the amount of oxygen in the water and prevent marine animals living beneath the carpet of plant matter from receiving their customary levels of sunlight. These twin effects kill some simple species outright; others that are higher on the food chain are also affected, but in different ways.

Larger animals such as sharks, for example, may experience sublethal effects: disease, deformities, and problems in reproducing. The kinds of pollutant released by some human activities, including industry and agriculture, combine easily with the oxygen component of water, as well as with the dissolved nitrogen present in most bodies

Sewage from a nearby factory gushes out of a drainage pipe and into the North Sea. Such pollution can have an indirect but serious effect on sharks.

of water, to form dangerous compounds. In the words of scientists Boyce Thorne-Miller and John Catena, "In water, the chemistry of pollution reacts readily with the chemistry of life." This unintentional mingling of reactive substances has an inevitable effect on sea animals, because toxic materials accumulate in the animals' bodies and cause disease.

The end results of chemical pollution are a serious decline in the health of an ecosystem and a reduction in the amount and diversity of species in that system. As Thorne-Miller and Catena point out, "It is a general rule that as pollution increases, the physiological and genetic health of marine populations declines, and eventually the number of species in the polluted ecosystem declines."

Toxic chemicals and more

Probably the most serious form of ocean pollution comes from pesticides, heavy metals, and other toxic chemicals released by industrial and agricultural operations. Pesticides and other chemicals flow into rivers or are absorbed into the atmosphere and, eventually, find their way into the ocean. All these pollutants can have indirect but significant effects on sharks.

Most toxic chemicals do not spread out widely in the ocean, so the most serious pollution occurs close to areas of intense industrial activity and heavy human settlement. The pollution level of a particular body of water depends on its size and its distance from these activities' sources of contaminants. The mouth of the St. Lawrence River, the Mediterranean Sea, and the Baltic Sea, are among the most polluted areas of the world's oceans. Other areas of heavy pollution include the North Sea, the coast of California, the Gulf of Mexico, and the inland sea of Japan.

In many parts of the world, raw, untreated sewage is pumped directly into the ocean, comprising another serious form of pollution. This sludge, along with other waste such as dredge spoils (silt that settles in channels and harbors that must be periodically dredged up), forms a sticky, thick layer on the bottom of the ocean that is lethal to virtually all the marine life around it.

Oil pollution

Oil pollution also takes a toll on sea life. Oil pollution may be catastrophic but short-lived, as in the cases of ship spills, pipeline breaks, and oil rig blowouts. More often, it is slow, long-term damage. For instance, diver and naturalist David K. Bulloch estimates that the amount of oil (mostly discarded motor oil) that leaches off land into the sea every year is six times greater than the amount spilled when the *Exxon Valdez* oil tanker ran aground in 1989, dumping nearly 11 million gallons of crude oil into the waters of Prince William Sound in Alaska.

Hot water that is discharged from nuclear plants, oil rigs, and other industrial operations is yet another hazard. These artificially created warm spots sometimes help certain species in the short run because the heated water provides better feeding grounds, but overall they kill off more fish than they help.

There is no research indicating that sharks are directly affected by these and other forms of pollution. But because such contamination damages the marine environment as a whole, and decreases the availability of populations of smaller prey species, sharks as top predators eventually will suffer.

Debris

Since the toxic chemicals of industrial and agricultural waste tend to remain in concentrated areas near the shore, sharks that live near coastlines are the most vulnerable to the effects of these pollutants on local ecosystems. However, the potential for long-term damage of even deep-ocean species is great from other sources of pollution.

Plastic containers and other forms of trash are regularly dumped from cargo ships and other vessels. This trash floats and can cover a widespread area. According to one estimate, merchant ships dump nearly half a million plastic containers into the open sea every day. No part of the ocean is unaffected by this debris, and it is regularly found even in such remote waters as the Antarctic.

Plastics and other trash can entangle, poison, or choke sharks and other sea life.

Sharks as well as other fish, sea mammals, seabirds, and sea turtles are threatened by such debris because it can entangle, poison, or choke them. David List, a spokesman for the U.S. Marine Commission, says that plastic containers and other trash are "like individual mines floating around the ocean just waiting for victims."

Many fishermen, for example, report encountering sharks that have thrust their snouts through plastic loops that once served as crating straps. A shark that has had this misfortune is trapped: unable to back out because it cannot swim backward, and unable to swim through the debris because the straps block its dorsal and pectoral fins.

Instead, as the shark grows, the straps tangled around its body begin to cut into its flesh. Sometimes the shark's skin partially heals over the strap, sealing the plastic immovably into the animal's body. Such injuries can seriously affect the shark's ability to feed, swim, and breathe.

Habitat destruction

A problem related to pollution is habitat destruction, the devastation of the regions where animals live, breed, and find food. Such destruction is typically caused by human activity, such as development, industry, or deforestation.

When trying to preserve an animal, experts argue, it is not enough to simply save individuals in a species. The species' home, and the unique ways in which it lives, must be preserved as well. Diane Ackerman, a distinguished natural history writer, asserts that "it's no use protecting an animal by itself; you have to protect its entire habitat. When people contribute to the Save the Panda campaign of the World Wildlife Fund, the money actually goes to protect the habitat of the pandas, not just the animal."

The same is true for sharks. Even if laws are passed banning the hunting of, for instance, the gray nurse shark, that species will remain endangered unless environmental laws are passed, as well, to protect regions essential to the shark's well-being, such as its normal breeding and feeding grounds.

Overall, the destruction of natural habitats is the single greatest threat to endangered wildlife. Land animals tend to be more seriously affected by habitat destruction than are animals that live in the sea. However, all sea animals—sharks included—are threatened by near-shore activity (usually performed by humans) that destroys portions of their homes.

Natural changes

Sometimes changes to habitats occur naturally, as wind and water erode a region's land, beach, or seafloor. Steep bluffs can crumble; new sand, silt, and stone can wash down from rivers. More and more frequently, however, change is due to human interference: alteration of the sea or shore due to the creation of new ports and harbor developments, building industrial and tourist facilities, and so on.

Coastal areas called wetlands are especially critical areas. Wetlands nurture the growth of algae and flowering plants such as eelgrass. These plants, in turn, provide food and shelter for a wide variety of small marine animals. Sharks feed on these smaller animals, which are lower on the food chain. Any disturbance of a wetlands area, therefore, could have a serious impact on sharks even if sharks are not directly affected by habitat destruction.

Roughly 50 percent of the original coastal wetlands of the United States were gone by the mid-1970s. Although the direct impact on sharks is not always well understood, many experts fear that such a large-scale change will affect sharks in years to come. "As human beings have populated the lands of the earth," note Boyce Thorne-Miller and John Catena, "we have pushed out other forms of life. It seemed to some that our impact must stop at the ocean's edge, but that has not proved to be so. . . . We have managed to impoverish, if not destroy, living ecosystems there as well."

Mangrove swamps, coral reefs, and the deep sea

Sometimes habitat destruction does have a direct and immediate impact on sharks. The serious decline in the number of lemon sharks off the coast of Florida, for instance, is in large part due to the loss of the mangrove swamps, which once served as nursery grounds for lemon pups. In recent years, however, much of Florida's mangrove swampland has been destroyed by developers, who have placed new homes and industrial facilities in these ecologically sensitive areas.

Another important but threatened habitat for sharks is the network of coral reefs throughout the warm, tropical waters of the world. The species that inhabit coral reefs

Florida developers have destroyed much of the mangrove swampland (right) that served as nursery grounds for lemon sharks (above).

are numerous and diverse. Each reef is the home of a wide variety of animals and plants, from tiny coral creatures and jellyfish to sponges, snails, algae, anemones, and millions of other tiny marine creatures. All these life-forms are interdependent, becoming food for progressively larger sea animals, including sharks.

Unfortunately, these delicate systems are being destroyed. In Malaysia, Thailand, Indonesia, the Philippines, and other parts of Southeast Asia, for example, large areas of coral reefs are being destroyed by blast fishing. This practice of detonating a variety of commercial, military, and homemade explosives in fish-laden waters is a very effective method of harvesting fish in the short term. In the long run, though, it destroys the reefs that fish and other species of plants and animals need for survival.

Effects unknown

For the time being, sharks that live in the deeper parts of the ocean are relatively safe from the effects of pollution and habitat destruction. If such practices as mining the seabed for minerals or burying waste in the seabed become widespread in the future, however, even deep-water sharks will be threatened.

Not much is known about how human activity in the deep sea will affect life there, but it is unrealistic to assume that the impact will be insignificant. Because scientists do not understand well—or even know anything about—many species of remote ocean plants and animals, it is impossible to know how serious the danger is, and how many species may face extinction.

The pioneer ocean researcher Jacques-Yves Cousteau feels that habitat destruction may be an even greater threat than direct pollution:

> We are dredging new marinas and commercial ports in places where [fish] have always come to feed, frolic, or breed. . . . New steamship lines, stepped-up urbanization of the coastline, breakneck industrial, residential, and recreational development, airports built out over the water, marinas, offshore drilling rigs—these and countless other manifestations of our destructive mania for "growth" are doing irreparable damage to the ocean environment in general and to . . . habitats in particular.

Sharks have flourished for hundreds of millions of years. But they will need to overcome pollution, habitat destruction, and other threatening conditions if they are to survive. It remains to be seen what the future will bring for them.

5

The Future for Sharks

IF SHARKS ARE to be saved, several issues will need to be addressed in the future. One crucial area, according to many experts, involves educating the public about sharks.

First, conservationists say, they must alert people to the endangered status of sharks. The next step will be to ensure that research about sharks continues, so that scientists can learn more about the rather mysterious creatures and the public will cease to view them primarily as threats to human life.

At the same time, shark advocates say, they will need to erase public apathy—the feeling that sharks are simply not worth saving. "The difficult task [Samuel] Gruber and other shark experts face," explains journalist Jane Bosveld, "is getting the public to care about the fate of creatures they love to hate, or as Gruber puts it, to care about 'the death fish from hell.' He and scientists have gotten the word out to the U.S. government, but legislation is slow in coming, primarily because there's not enough pressure from the public."

Save the Sharks?

Educating the public and easing popular fear of sharks is a primary challenge.

Around the world, many organizations and individuals are sympathetic to, and interested in, protecting wild or rare animals. For instance, there are well-organized and well-publicized movements to save the whales, to protect panda bears, and to shelter elephants and gorillas. But few people actively work to save the sharks, and most are unaware that sharks are in danger.

People often fear what they do not understand, and sharks are often a source of dread for this very reason. By educating the public about the dangers sharks face and their crucial role in ocean ecology, conservationists hope to make an important step toward influencing government agencies. These agencies might then be persuaded to institute measures to protect sharks.

What is needed, many experts say, is a "Save the Sharks" campaign similar to the effort on behalf of whales in the 1970s and 1980s. "Save the Whales," the massive grassroots project that formed a major part of the modern environmental movement, is credited with helping to raise the public's awareness about endangered whales and the earth's ecology in general.

In order to protect sharks, conservationists first need to improve sharks' fearsome image. Many organizations have sponsored snorkeling expeditions as part of the campaign to educate the public.

Scientists hope that the knowledge they are gaining about sharks will contribute to promoting public sympathy for the plight of these primitive, sometimes threatening creatures. As researchers learn more about sharks, they are better able to understand what lies behind the animals' fierceness—and the public's fear. "Sharks are getting hammered everywhere around the world," according to Gail Van Dykhuizen, a research biologist at the Monterey Bay Aquarium. "It's just that you don't tend to hear about it because they're not warm, fuzzy animals."

Peter Benchley, who did much to amplify the modern fear of sharks when he wrote *Jaws*, says that his portrayal of a mindless undersea killer was based on the information available at the time. New information that scientists have developed about sharks led Benchley to change his opinion, however, and he now says: "I couldn't write *Jaws* today. The extensive new knowledge of sharks would make it impossible for me to create, in good conscience, a villain of the magnitude and malignity [evilness] of the original."

Poster child for terror?

Researchers and environmentalists who are concerned about dwindling shark populations hope to reverse or slow the trend by, for example, mounting a campaign to increase public understanding of sharks and awareness of the problems that might result from their disappearance.

This will not be an easy task. Sharks lack the appeal of some other endangered animals; they are not cute like panda bears, for instance, or apparently friendly like whales. As writer Jane Bosveld puts it, "When it comes to sympathy for endangered species, the shark is at the bottom of the list. This poster child for terror rarely inspires goodwill."

Nonetheless, conservationists hope to increase public sympathy by replacing the many prevailing myths about sharks with basic truths about the animals. By developing an appreciation of sharks for what they are—fascinating, kingly creatures almost perfectly adapted to a complex ocean environment—advocates may be able to provide a foundation for better understanding.

Unfortunately for those eager to preserve sharks, future protective legislation will probably be slow in coming. For instance, the International Union for the Conservation of Nature (IUCN), the agency that administers CITES, has been slow to add new species to its endangered list.

So far, the most effective legislation affecting sharks has been in the form of local laws that protect specific species, such as ordinances protecting the gray nurse shark in southern Australia and the great white shark in South Africa. Elsewhere, activists have been making slow but sure progress. Journalist Catherine Dold elaborates: "Considering that [in 1991] few people gave sharks a second thought, environmentalists have made considerable progress pressing for shark fishery controls."

One important turning point came in 1994, when environmentalists persuaded the hundred-plus nations that have signed CITES to assemble new data on biological and trade issues affecting shark fisheries worldwide. That same year,

Conservationists contend that because sharks are seen as vicious predators, they do not receive as much public support as other endangered wildlife.

As the public becomes more aware of the threatened status of sharks, measures are slowly being taken to protect the endangered species.

a major conservation organization, the World Wildlife Fund, sponsored an investigation into the international trade in the fins, cartilage, meat, skin, and oil of sharks.

A ban?

Advocates of controls on shark fishing hope that the IUCN will use the results of the wildlife fund's investigation to create a ban restricting trade in all products made from sharks. No species of shark is currently protected by an international ban comparable to those now in effect on other commodities from endangered species, such as folk medicines from rhinoceros horns and ivory from elephant tusks. However, the World Wildlife Fund investigation is not scheduled to be finished soon, and serious controls on trade could not be expected for several years after the study's completion.

Some experts argue, meanwhile, that there is strong evidence that bans alone are not adequate solutions. This, they say, is because laws work only if they can be enforced.

Policing the trade in endangered species is extremely difficult. The merchandise is so valuable that smugglers and traders take extraordinary measures to cover their activities. In addition, poachers and others involved in black-market (illegal) trade in endangered species sometimes have the unofficial cooperation of corrupt personnel in government agencies. Bans on ivory and rhino horns have slowed the trade in those animal parts somewhat, but it has been impossible to completely stop poachers.

A ban on shark fins and cartilage may be as difficult to police as the bans on ivory and rhino horns. Even if such a ban could be properly enforced, some experts fear, it may be too late. Many shark populations are in such serious trouble right now, they say, that there is no time to lose. According to Merry Camhi, an ecologist for the National Audubon Society, "We really can't wait until the information comes together before we start managing [shark populations] more effectively."

Controls

In the United States, environmentalists are lobbying for stricter controls than those represented by the 1993 guidelines of the National Marine Fisheries Service. These limited restrictions on shark hunting, conservationists say, do not go far enough in setting caps on catches and do not cover enough species of sharks.

Another primary government agency responsible for monitoring ocean life, the National Oceanographic and Atmospheric Administration (NOAA), plans to issue guidelines limiting shark catches within U.S. fishing waters. Nancy Foster, a spokeswoman for NOAA, presents an encouraging position statement: "We recognize that shark populations are in need of strong management measures to help them rebound to safe population numbers." However, the NOAA guidelines are not yet complete, and it is not clear how they would differ from the NMFS guidelines.

Conservationists warn that if stricter measures are not taken soon, commercial and sport fishing for shark will follow commercial whaling to extinction. Fishing for whales was once a huge industry, but in recent years it has essentially died out. Strong international pressure to protect whales was partly responsible for the demise of commercial whaling, but whalers had nearly fished their way out of a living at about the same time that the Save the Whales campaign gained public recognition.

The same thing may happen to shark fishermen. But some biologists offer hope that the worst-case scenario may be avoided if adequate controls are passed within the next few years. The key is to limit the industry carefully. As Jack Musick, the shark expert at the Virginia Institute of Marine Science, states: "You've got to have the will to manage [shark fisheries] for the long-term, not for immediate gratification. It's to the fishermen's advantage to have some assurance that the animals will be there year after year to provide them a living."

The future of the ESA

There is controversy and uncertainty over the future of the Endangered Species Act, the law that protects endangered species in the United States. The current moratorium, or ban, on adding new animals—including any species of sharks—to the list of animals protected by this act is a particular cause of concern.

The ban, which was proposed by conservative lawmakers, benefits developers, fishermen, and others who profit from the commercial use of land and resources. One major sponsor of the ban, Senator Kay Bailey Hutchison of Texas, sees it as a means to "strike a balance between the need to preserve species, and [the need] to protect private property rights of private land owners."

As a result of the moratorium, no new species have been added to the ESA list since 1995, and over 240 potentially endangered species—animals that were awaiting listing—were specifically excluded. According to Jamie Clark, the U.S. Fish and Wildlife Service's assistant director of Eco-

logical Services, "At this point the listings program for the Fish and Wildlife Service is entirely shut down."

Environmentalists, meanwhile, hope to restore the effectiveness of the Endangered Species Act by enlisting public support to influence politicians. Clark offers the following explanation for this strategy: "I don't think that the majority of the congressional delegation understands that the American public is against extinction and that the American public supports species conservation."

Legislation like the ESA depends on public support, public support depends on education, and education depends on continuing research. The more researchers know about sharks, the more the public can appreciate the creatures for what they are. As British research scientist Rodney Steel asserts, "Large predatory species [such as sharks] are . . . no less dangerous to swimmers or surfers for having become better understood. But the motivation for their attacks is now more comprehensible."

A great white shark shows its teeth as it passes by an underwater camera. While the great white shark and seven other species are listed as endangered, environmentalists believe there are many other sharks that should be added to this list.

A diver tests a glove that is made from a material that is impenetrable to sharks' teeth. Equipment such as this has allowed researchers to get closer than ever to sharks.

The future of shark research

The development of sophisticated undersea equipment has assisted scientists who seek to enter the world under the sea and record its secrets. No longer do they need to rely on dead sharks or sluggish aquarium specimens. Steel shark cages from which divers make observations and take photographs, chain-mail protective suits, and other innovations let researchers get closer than ever before. Even with this equipment, however, shark research remains too often a difficult, dangerous, and poorly funded branch of science.

New techniques and equipment are needed to give observers greater access to sharks in their natural environment. One major problem that remains to be solved, for instance, is that of tracking sharks across time and over long distances. The use of underwater ultrasonics has been an important technological advance in this regard, since ultrasonic equipment allows observers to closely follow the movements of individual fish. Other relatively new tools for shark research include the small one- or two-person submarines called submersibles, and advanced apparatus for underwater video and photography. These devices aid researchers in gathering data on sharks as they interact with the ocean environment.

Researchers hope that such advances will help them attain a better understanding of the behavior patterns of sharks. They also hope to learn exactly how specific problems such as pollution and habitat destruction affect sharks. There is evidence now that sharks are affected by these developments, but not enough proof to support very many solid conclusions. As Boyce Thorne-Miller and John Catena, staff scientists for the environmental group Friends of the Earth, note:

Though advances in technology have allowed researchers to get closer to their subjects, studying sharks is still a difficult and dangerous science.

Many marine biologists who have observed natural marine communities over a period of time believe they have seen significant declines in populations of some species. But they do not have data to confirm or refute these impressions. More field data is needed if we are to determine the [future] status of marine species [such as sharks]. . . . [W]e must abandon our assumptions and gather more facts.

The cartilage craze continues

Research into the possible medicinal properties of shark cartilage remains highly controversial, sparking concerns in at least two areas. Many conservationists and shark biologists worry about the well-being of sharks, should reliable proof emerge that drugs obtainable only from shark cartilage could benefit humankind. Many doctors and medical investigators, on the other hand, are concerned about potential damage to serious cancer research due to the hype and pseudoscience that accompany much of the media coverage of the research in this area.

I. William Lane, the man who started the cartilage craze, recently got permission to perform clinical human trials in the United States. He hopes that these tests—which involve Benefin, the compound he manufactures and markets—will prove his claims of anticancer properties for shark cartilage. Lane compares his situation to a court trial: "The FDA [Food and Drug Administration] has allowed me to go to the jury. I will either be a hero or a dud."

Lane's critics, however, worry that in the meantime the worldwide demand for cartilage is adding to the already difficult survival problems faced by sharks. Indeed, there is evidence that in economically depressed countries such as Costa Rica, large numbers of sharks are being killed specifically for cartilage. This is at least partly because cartilage harvesting is one of the few profitable businesses open to fishermen in some less affluent coastal regions. Journalist Catherine Dold quotes the owner of a Costa Rican fish factory who believes that the cartilage craze has played an important role in making the shark an attractive catch: "Because they can sell everything, fishermen are dedicating themselves to sharks." Dold adds:

The rationale is that sharks will be harvested for their meat and fins anyway. But there is little doubt that shark fishing is increasing as cartilage gains in popularity. [The factory owner] reports that 50 percent more of the fish he buys are sharks than five years ago, even as the fishermen complain that they have to go farther and farther to find them.

Some cancer specialists acknowledge that research on shark cartilage may someday prove useful in the fight against cancer. But by most projections, investigators are decades away from producing solid results. Meanwhile, some fear that the perception that such studies are questionable science will damage the funding of more conventional scientific research. The research still to be done before cartilage medicine might be safely given to the public is highly complex. As researcher Judah Folkman of Harvard Medical School points out, it is "like going from Kitty Hawk to the moon."

Years of carefully controlled testing remain before it can be said definitely whether shark cartilage is a miracle cure or a cruel hoax. At present, a small amount of government-approved testing is under way in addition to Lane's trials. Stuart Leimer, a doctor at the Cancer Center at St. Barnabas Medical Center in Livingston, New Jersey, is one of the physicians who has been supervising these tests. Many of his colleagues are skeptical, but he is trying to keep an open mind. "Instead of saying it doesn't work," he suggests, "let's give it a chance and see what it can do."

Alternatives to commercial fishing

Some shark experts hold out hope for future advances in enterprises called shark farms—large-scale, commercial operations that breed sharks for human consumption. Development of a successful shark farm industry could help maintain a high shark population while ensuring the availability of these fish as a resource for people. The concept is similar to that of growing trees on tree farms, as renewable resources. Certain kinds of fish, such as salmon, have been successfully bred in captivity in a process sometimes called aquaculture. So far, however, experimental applications of aquaculture techniques to the raising of sharks have not been successful. This is partly because sharks' size and potential for inflicting injury make them difficult and dangerous to handle. Moreover, their need to move constantly calls for pens or holding cages vastly larger than usually required, hence much more expensive. Another problem to be overcome is the need to process fresh shark meat even more quickly than other kinds of fish to prevent spoilage.

But the most important reason for the lack of success so far of attempts to breed sharks in captivity is the animals' long reproductive cycle. Sharks grow slowly, taking years to reach sexual maturity. Also, they give birth, on average, only once every few years, and then only to a single pup or, at best, a few.

Obviously, then, a successful shark farm would have to be managed very conservatively, with small amounts of sharks harvested over a very long period of time. According to Rodney Steel, "Because sharks are such slow breeders, no large-scale commercial shark fishery established in any one locality has ever proved viable [an economic success]. In a matter of months, or at best a few years, the shark stocks are fished out and they take decades to regenerate."

Controlled sport fishing and ecotourism

A major justification for continuing commercial shark fishing is that it provides jobs. The shark fishing industry argues that if a ban is put in place, its members will have no way to make a living. Conservationists suggest two possible alternative business ventures that might be helpful.

One would be the development of a carefully controlled and monitored sport fishing industry that used strict catch limits or a catch-and-release rule to maintain high population levels. This approach offers the potential to provide a good living for former fishermen who become guides. According to journalist Ted Williams, a recreational shark fishery for the Atlantic Coast and Gulf of Mexico alone might be expected to generate as much as $130 million a year.

Another possible economic base for fishing communities is shark watching, a variation on ecotourism. A very popular form of recreation in recent years, ecotourism is organized travel to environmentally sensitive regions, with an emphasis on animal watching and identification rather than hunting.

Organized whale watching is already a multimillion-dollar enterprise for coastal communities that once relied on killing whales. While shark watching is not being done on as large a scale, the potential is impressive.

Shark watching

Some tropical communities are already actively developing shark-watching industries. In the Maldive Islands in the Indian Ocean, for instance, underwater shark watchers currently generate almost $25 million a year for local businesses. Thousands of divers visit shark populations in other parts of the world as well. The whale sharks that swim off Western Australia's Ningaloo Reef are popular for watching, as are the reef sharks, black-tipped sharks, lemons, and hammerheads that thrive in the Bahamas. "Ecotourism based on shark watching is big business all over the world," Williams claims.

These operations are designed to ensure that divers can see sharks close up and identify them under conditions that are safe for humans and sharks alike. Spotter planes track the whereabouts of sharks and lure them to target areas by means of frozen morsels called chumsicles (after "chum," the traditional attractant consisting of chopped bait fish and other ingredients). Regulations control the number of vessels allowed in the water around prime spotting areas, to make sure that the sharks and other marine creatures are not scared away. Sometimes guides manage to attach tags to individual sharks so that spotters can easily identify the various species.

Advocates say that the economic potential of shark watching is far greater than that of simply catching the creatures. The amount of money ecotourists spend to see a shark, in other words, is much larger than the worth of the shark as a product. As Williams notes, "To a commercial fisherman [in the Bahamas] these animals would be worth something like $50 each, but to Walker's Cay [one of the Bahama islands] the figure is $10,000, according to Gary Adkison, who started the shark dives five years ago."

The future of biodiversity

Even if conservationists succeed in having strict legislation passed to protect sharks, the problems facing sharks will not be over. Nor will sharks be completely safe even if commercial fishing stops completely, or if the ocean's pollution levels drop dramatically. This is because habitat destruction will continue to endanger them, along with the many thousands of other species of animal and plant life that have evolved over 3 billion years.

A diver uses food to lure a reef shark as another shark circles around him. Shark-watching industries are developing in some parts of the world as a profitable alternative to shark fishing.

Sharks have survived and prospered in the world's oceans for hundreds of millions of years, outlasting the dinosaurs, the saber-toothed cat, and the earliest humans. Perhaps they will outlast modern humans as well.

If sharks die out, the planet will lose a crucial link in the biodiversity and ecology of the ocean. And people will lose something, as well: the opportunity to see these awe-inspiring predators in the wild.

In the words of journalist Todd Preston, "To lose sharks to carelessness and greed would be an inexcusable crime. . . . We have nothing to gain from the loss of the sharks, but everything to lose."

83

Glossary

angiogenesis: The process in which new blood vessels are attracted to cancerous growths. Angiogenesis is the basis of a controversial cancer treatment using shark cartilage.

biodiversity: The variety of life-forms in a natural community.

bycatch: Accidental catches in the nets or lines of fishermen. Sharks often end up as bycatch of fishermen who are after tuna or other kinds of fish.

cartilage: Tough bodily tissue that connects the bones of people and other animals. In sharks, the skeletal framework itself is made of cartilage, not bones.

CITES: The Convention of International Trade in Endangered Species of Wild Fauna and Flora, an international treaty banning import and export of endangered species.

ecosystem: The interrelated complex of life-forms in an environment.

endangered species: A species in danger of becoming extinct in all or part of its normal habitats.

Endangered Species Act (ESA): A U.S. law passed in 1973 and subsequently amended that defines "endangered" and "threatened" species and establishes a formal structure to protect them.

food chain: The series of links between animals that eat other animals. A typical food chain down might describe how a shark eats smaller fish, the fish eat mussels, and the mussels eat plankton. Food chains that are very complicated are sometimes called food webs because so many animals are part of an interconnected system.

habitat: The region, including land, water, vegetation, and air, that a species needs for survival.

overfishing: The taking from the sea of so many fish that the population of one or more species declines sharply or vanishes. Overfishing is a serious danger for certain kinds of fish, including sharks, that reproduce slowly.

oviparous: The term describing sharks or other creatures that lay eggs.

ovoviviparous: The term describing sharks whose eggs develop and hatch inside the female; the firstborn shark pups feed on unfertilized eggs in the womb and later eat other pups of the same litter.

poaching: The hunting or trapping of wildlife illegally.

species: A group of related animals or plants that can breed with members of their own kind but not (usually) with others.

threatened species: A species at risk of becoming endangered if it is not protected.

viviparous: The term used to describe sharks and other animals that develop their young live inside the female; as in mammals, unborn sharks of viviparous species are fed by a placenta.

Organizations to Contact

The Cousteau Society
930 W. 21st St.
Norfolk, VA 23517
(804) 627-7547
An environmental group founded by Jacques-Yves Cousteau, a pioneer undersea explorer.

Defenders of Wildlife
1244 19th St. NW
Washington, DC 20036
(202) 659-9510
A conservation group that focuses on endangered animals.

EarthWatch
680 Mt. Auburn St.
P.O. Box 403N
Watertown, MA 02272
(617) 926-8200
An organization devoted to direct action aimed at preserving wilderness and animals.

Environmental Defense Fund
257 Park Ave.
New York, NY 10010
A group that raises and distributes money to protect the environment.

International Union for the Conservation of Nature and Natural Resources
1400 16th St. NW
Washington, DC 20036
(202) 797-5454

The U.S. office of the international organization that administers CITES.

National Audubon Society
950 Third Ave.
New York, NY 10022
(212) 832-3200
One of the oldest and best-known conservation groups in the United States.

National Marine Fisheries Service
1315 East-West Highway
Silver Spring, MD 20910
(301) 713-2347
One of the branches of the federal government responsible for monitoring shark populations and managing protective laws.

National Wildlife Federation
1412 16th St. NW
Washington, DC 20036
(202) 797-6800
A large conservation group dedicated to protecting wild animals.

Sierra Club
730 Polk St.
San Francisco, CA 94109
(415) 776-2211
Like the Audubon Society, one of the oldest and best-known conservation groups in America.

U.S. Fish and Wildlife Service
Publications Unit
Washington, DC 20240
Like all the organizations mentioned here, this group provides information about endangered animals.

World Wildlife Fund
1250 24th St. NW
Washington, DC 20037
(202) 293-4800
The U.S. headquarters of a large international environmental organization.

Suggestions for Further Reading

Wyatt Blassingame, *The Wonders of Sharks*. New York: Dodd, Mead, 1984. A good, clearly written introduction to sharks, though not with much detail.

Guido Dingerkus, *The Shark Watchers' Guide*. New York: Messner, 1985. A general overview written by a noted shark expert. Good for basic reference.

Ron Hirschi, *Save Our Oceans and Coasts*. New York: Delacorte, 1993. A brief but useful introduction to how marine wildlife and habitats are threatened, written under the auspices of the National Audubon Society.

Doug Perrine, *Sharks*. Stillwater, MN: Voyageur Press, 1995. A well-organized and clearly written introduction to the subject, with an especially good section on the biology of sharks.

Don C. Reed, *Sevengill: The Shark and Me*. New York: Knopf/Sierra Club, 1986. An interesting memoir by a professional diver who worked with sharks at a zoological park in California.

Alvin, Virginia, and Robert Silverstein, *Saving Endangered Animals*. Hillside, NJ: Enslow Publishers, 1993. Although this book does not mention sharks specifically, it is a good introduction to the subject of endangered species.

Works Consulted

Diane Ackerman, *The Rarest of the Rare*. New York: Random House, 1995. Intelligent, well-written essays on endangered species by one of America's best natural history writers.

Douglas Adams, *Last Chance to See*. New York: Harmony Books, 1990. A book about rare and endangered animals by the author of *The Hitchhiker's Guide to the Galaxy*.

Peter Benchley, "Misunderstood Monsters," *Smithsonian*, April 1995. A magazine piece by the author of *Jaws*, reflecting on how the novel affected the public's perception of sharks and how new information about them changed the point of view of Benchley himself.

Jane Bosveld, "When the Tables Are Turned," *Omni*, November 1994. A brief but informative magazine piece about the dangers that humans present to sharks.

David K. Bulloch, *The Underwater Naturalist*. New York: Lyons & Burford, 1991. A useful but densely written book about exploring the natural sciences underwater.

José I. Castro, *The Sharks of North American Waters*. College Station: Texas A&M University Press, 1983. A detailed and mostly technical manual, written for scientists and fishermen.

Richard Conniff, "From Jaws to Laws," *Smithsonian*, May 1993. A magazine article about pending legislation to protect sharks.

Julianne Couch and Tracey Rembert, "Back from the Brink," *E: the Environmental Magazine*, July/August 1996. A brief magazine piece about the fight to preserve endangered sharks.

Jacques-Yves and Philippe Cousteau, *The Shark*. London: Cassell, 1970. A book by the famous undersea explorer and one of his sons. In alerting the world to the treasures of the sea, the Cousteaus were pioneers of the movement to save endangered species.

Leigh Dayton, "Save the Sharks," *New Scientist*, June 15, 1991. A fairly technical magazine article about the reasons behind shark conservation efforts.

Catherine Dold, "Shark Therapy," *Discover,* April 1996. An informative and balanced article on the use of sharks for medical research. Its focus is on the controversial shark cartilage treatment for cancer and on the massive cartilage-harvesting industry in Costa Rica.

Richard Ellis, *Monsters of the Sea*. New York: Knopf, 1994. A complex book about myths, legends, and realities of sea monsters, written by a distinguished expert on ocean life.

Philip Elmer-Dewitt, "Are Sharks Becoming Extinct?" *Time*, March 4, 1991. A brief overview of shark endangerment.

Mary Emanoil, ed., *Encyclopedia of Endangered Species*. Washington, DC: Gale Research, 1996. A reference book published in coordination with the IUCN, the international agency that monitors endangered species.

Cal Fussman, "Hunting the Hunter," *Life*, August 1991. A magazine piece on sport fishing for sharks.

Michael Glantz, "Many Species Today in Danger of Being Hunted to Extinction," Knight-Ridder/Tribune News Service, January 5, 1996. A newspaper article about the growing numbers of extinct or endangered species.

Peter Goadby and George Bell, "Predators in Peril," *Outdoor Life*, January 1992. A brief piece that presents catch-and-release sport fishing as one way to conserve shark populations.

Suzanne Kingsmill, *Vanishing Wildlife*. New York: Gallery Books, 1991. A large-format book, well written and well illustrated, that serves as a good overview to the problems of wildlife endangerment.

Lynette Lamb, "Fish Gotta Swim and Birds Gotta Fly," *Utne Reader*, September/October 1994. A brief article about the growing number of endangered species.

R. D. Lawrence, *Shark! Nature's Masterpiece*. Shelburne, VT: Chapters, 1985. A volume in the Curious Naturalist Series, written by a veteran natural history writer.

Rosie Mestel, "Sharks' Healing Powers," *Natural History*, September 1996. A highly technical article that focuses on the possible reasons for immune systems of sharks to be especially strong, and how current medical research may someday help humans.

Farley Mowat, *Sea of Slaughter*. Toronto, Canada: McClelland and Stewart, 1984. A book by the distinguished naturalist and conservationist that focuses on the northeastern seaboard of Canada and the United States.

Michael Parfit, "Diminishing Returns," *National Geographic*, November 1995. A lengthy article with wonderful photos that focuses on the diminishing numbers of fish in the sea.

Rodney Steel, *Sharks of the World*. New York: Facts on File, 1985. A good and detailed work by a British research scientist, very useful as a reference tool despite its dry style.

Edward Stern, "Endangered Species List: Extinct?" *Mother Earth News*, August/September 1996. A brief magazine piece about the moratorium on declaring new endangered species.

John D. Stevens, ed., *Sharks.* New York: Facts on File, 1987. An extremely detailed overview, with contributions from many distinguished experts and excellent photos.

Boyce Thorne-Miller and John Catena, *The Living Ocean.* Washington, DC: Island Press, 1991. A densely written but excellent book, by staff scientists for the environmental group Friends of the Earth, that focuses on the importance of biodiversity in the ocean.

Ted Williams, "Attack on the Sharks," *Audubon,* July/August 1996. A lengthy magazine piece that examines the reasons behind the decline in U.S. shark populations and the obstacles faced by conservationists and scientists trying to pass legislation to preserve endangered species.

Index

About the Author

Adam Woog is the author of many books for adults and young adults, on subjects ranging from museums and inventions to Amelia Earhart and Louis Armstrong. He lives in Seattle, Washington, with his wife and young daughter.

Picture Credits